MW00760151

Rebel

A Collection of Poems by

Tom Rohe

Goblin Fern Press

Madison, Wisconsin

Copyright © 2005 by Tom Rohe

All rights reserved.

Published by:
Goblin Fern Press, Inc.
3809 Mineral Point Road
Madison, WI 53705
www.goblinfernpress.com
Toll-free: 888-670-BOOK (2665)

ISBN-10: 1-59598-031-8
ISBN-13: 978-1-59598-031-1
LCCN: 2005930565

Printed in the United States.
First Printing

Dedicated
to Tiana and Jonathan,

May they grow up to become
independent, free thinking
adults

Table of Contents

Table of Contents, Continued

Preface

When the decision was made to take these poems out of the base-ment and publish them, *Rebel* immediately came to mind for a title. These poems were written between the fall of 1980, when I was 17 years old, and the spring of 1989, when I was 26. During this period of my life, I was always rebelling against something.

Poems 1 through 8 were written when I was a senior in high school. *The Deer* was a rebellion against the hunting culture of northern Wisconsin, of which my dad and brothers were a part. *Alcohol Nights* expresses the exhilaration of rebelling against au-thority through underage drinking. *I Stand Alone* was a rebellion against my peers. They seemed to share the same religious and philosophic values of their parents, values which I rejected.

Written 19 years before the Columbine school massacre, *Life Inside the Shell* describes the very intense, dark moods, which adolescents can into fall from time to time. *Too Late* was my re-action to the suicide of a high school classmate.

In the fall of 1981, I entered the University of Wisconsin and the issues changed. Poems 9 through 26 were written during my first five semesters in college.

The *Patti* poems arose from my first infatuation, involving Patti P., a young woman from Chicago. In the summer of 1982, my parents owned a campground in northern Wisconsin. Patti and her family stayed at a cottage for a week. Upon leaving at the end of the week, Patti broke into tears because she would no longer be seeing me. This took me completely by surprise. She was very attractive, nice to talk to, intelligent, and one year older than me. We hugged, kissed and promised to write.

This started an intense, long distance romance carried on through love letters, long telephone calls and constant preparations to see each other. We were always planning to see each other "next month," but our plans were consistently disrupted by circumstances. Eight months after the tearful sendoff, without ever having had the chance to see each other again, she let me know that she was back with an old boyfriend. She apologized for ever giving me hope. I was devastated.

I wrote 28 poems about the situation, seven of which appear in this book. In *For Patti VI: As the Curtain Falls*, I cut apart portions of other poems to form a new poem. Dissecting the poems was therapeutic, as I felt like I was killing the infatuation. *without her* is the postscript.

In college, I became politically active and wrote a number of political poems. *I Cry for Nations Caged in Red* and *Reaganomics Soup* will have to take their niche in time. *A Shot of Vodka in the Morning* was my protest against the glorification of conservatism, which was everywhere in the 1980s.

party poems is a depiction of high school/college party life. It is a world where alcohol flows freely and members of each sex view the opposite sex as sexual objects. As we get older, we shake our heads at such behavior, familiar with the dangers inherent therein. However, one still has to admire the spirit of adventure and uninhibited freedom. It is this spirit, which the poem celebrates.

In the spring of 1984, I took a poetry workshop at the University, producing poems 27 through 33. *Black Cross with Red Sky* was inspired by the Georgia O'Keefe painting of the same name. *elegy written in a country churchyard: 1983* was my response to the Thomas Gray classic, one of the most beautiful poems in the English language, but one with which I have a philosophic disagreement.

Progress is a palindrome, which reads the same frontwards and backwards. It is the first of several poems that deal with the conflict between corporate culture and humanity.

in the beginning is an atheistic/paganistic genesis story.

The Idealist's Song: Walking the Streets of Neenah, Wisconsin was my response to the assignment that week, which was to write a sonnet. I completely submerged the form to make it appear as free verse, rebelling against the conventional form, similar to how the character in the poem rebels against a conventional life. One can only tell that it is a sonnet by underlining every tenth syllable.

After *Reaganomics Soup*, I did not write another poem for two and a half years. The pressure of having to produce a new poem almost every week for the workshop completely burned me out. Instead, I concentrated on maintaining good grades for law school applications, and the study of law, itself.

I began writing poetry again in the fall of 1986, when I was a second year student at Duke University School of Law in Durham, North Carolina. Poems 34 through 39 were written during my last two years of law school. Poems 40 through 43 were written during my first year of legal practice.

The Old Man Begins Writing Poetry and *Flies* arose from the pressure to conform to a corporate culture, which I began to experience as I interviewed with law firms. *Escape Into the Snow* was a direct rebellion against my first law firm.

in the mountains of north carolina and *prayer to the moon* are escapist, philosophic and spiritual. They are essentially atheistic prayers, depicting the deep, abiding love of nature that I feel is an inherent part of all of us.

Morning on a Tributary Which Flows Into the Eno reveals nature to be restless and full of danger. This, to a certain extent, is mirrored in our own lives.

Other poems from this time frame simply describe experiences of young adulthood, such as babysitting, *To Scott Van Zeeland, my nephew*, an unsatisfactory relationship, *"Just Friends" Having Sex*, or the desperation of loneliness, *Single at 24*.

The volume ends with *Sunset Over the Gravestones*, a philosophic piece. After this poem, I stopped writing poetry. Several circumstances combined to produce this result.

I joined a new law firm in 1989, the firm that I am still with today. I became established in my legal career. I found it impossible to transition from the logical cause-and-effect thinking of a lawyer to the free-for-all, emotional thought process of a poet.

Furthermore, in December 1990, I met my wife, and we now have two beautiful children. The emotional lability, which served as the creative force for many of my poems, is now gone.

It recently dawned on me that these poems should not just be sitting idle. I decided to take them from the basement and place them into this volume, for whoever would like to read them, as a tribute to the challenges, frailties and rebelliousness of youth.

Tom Rohe
February 2005

Rebel

The Deer

The strong but beautiful body walks among the woods
On his never ending search for food.
The reds and golds of autumn fall all around him
As he slowly makes his way through the maple.
Alert yet calm,
He moves gently as he pleases,
Stopping every now and then
To listen to the forest music.
Sunlight making its way through the trees
Shines softly on his head
As if to show off what Mother Nature has done.
As if obeying a God given command
The whole body slowly breaks into a run
        And he runs.
Strong of heart, fleet of foot,
The deer runs gently through the woods
Bouncing lightly among the oak and the pine.
"Peace on earth" he seems to say
As he runs in the direction of his destination
And the reds and golds fall behind him
small floating vessels on a sea of air.

Suddenly, terror strikes the autumn sky
As a shot is heard through the trees.
I run as fast as my legs can pump
Just to find the deer sprawled on the ground.
Agonizing panic is in his eye
And he looks at me as if to say "Why?"
He thrashes his legs, kicking up mud
In one last attempt to restore life
But the bullet sinks deeper into his side
As each second goes by.

I want desperately to help him
But it is all in vain.
He stretches his muscles one last time.
Then death replaces what once was joy.

The deer had the freedom
Which all men would like to experience.
Yet, man took away his gift
Just so he could have a trophy.

Dreamland

Nighttime calling, lie down to sleep,
Enter a world of star dusted dreams.
Long lost memories of a distant time
Spring out from their hiding places inside of the mind.
A childhood friend, a basketball game
A swim in the brook, a walk in the rain
A snowmobile ride, a fourth grade class
The blue eyed beauty on the green grass.
And as consciousness begins to fall
Hopes and dreams begin to rise.
They're fulfilled before one's very eyes.
Tomorrow, when the buzz signifies the new day
A new course will be set,
One which will take us to the threshold of a dream.
But, tonight, all that awaits is unconsciousness
Which sweeps all thoughts away.
We enter into a world of helium balloons and cherry pies
Of cops and robbers and paper moons
Of love and hate and life and death
Of childlike fears, hopes and desires.
The unfocused projector plays in our head
Showing us the way.

Alcohol Nights

Alcohol Nights
A rocket ride to the top of the sky
A jettison out into the air
A gradual falling back down to earth
Where the pine scent forest meets the starry waters.
Alcohol Nights
Scamper around in search of a dream
Follow a hawk to the top of a tree
Plunge into unknowns of other people's minds
Jump back out an educated man.
Alcohol Nights
Catching love by the tail's end
Swept into paradise by a stroke of fate
Climbing up the scale at a snail's pace
Sliding back down with the passage of time.
Alcohol Nights
Rebellious and alive, strong and free
Windswept fires of underage heaven
Doused out at the chiming of twelve
By parental worries and talk of hell.
Alcohol Nights
A chance to reach an enchanted star
To become a comet without an orbit
To become a free man before one's time
To live and love and grow as we wish.
Alcohol Nights
Where there are no boundaries
Where there are no chains
Where all can be real
In a young man's dreams.

Life Inside the Shell

Optimism crashes on a newly built brick wall.
Depression comes on so powerfully strong.
Damned desperation screwing up my mind.
I dive into the shell before I get stung.
Sounds waves from my vocal cords are unable
to reach an ear.
So, I write, and write, and write, and write, and
guzzle too much beer.
Dreams and hopes are mutilated time after time.
I can no longer see clearly because it's raining
inside of my mind.

        It's time to attack.
        It's time to get all of you back.
    Knives, whips, guns, guillotine
    Which weapon shall I choose?
    Burning, torture, decapitation
    Which method shall I use?
Never again will I put up with such abuse.
You'd better start to run because I am on the loose.
    Dirty, vengeful, despicable scoundrels
    You will meet your just rewards.
    Cheating, lying, hating fools
    Prepare yourself for war.
It doesn't matter who you are, all of you are the same.
I'll kill you no matter what your color, age or name.
So, look out world, I'm going to bust out of my shell.
Then, everything you love will become a flaming hell.

Spring Song

The lush green lawn invades my acid thoughts
Prevailing.
A breeze accompanies spring's new born scene
Soothing.
The winter chill has given way
To long cool walks late in the day.
The world has come alive once again.

Backyard ponds full of winter's tears
Reflecting
Sunlit rays bouncing to the sky
Shining.
The winter snows are memory
Which melted into harmony
Reflections bright which stretch across the yard.

Little children run and play and hide
Laughing.
The chirps of birds signal thoughts of freedom
Calling.
The music of youth sprays the air
Forecasting summer's lively fair.
A world has gone; A world has come; let us enjoy today.

Somewhere In the Night

Freaks on the corners, dressed in denim jackets
Trying to convince the world of their sin
Walk toughly to the park
To score some pot and beer.
Sweet young lovers, arm in arm
Walk slowly into a house
To create a world of romance and fantasy
With kisses meant to warm.
Red-eyed beer patrons cruise in a car
Screaming, yelling, swearing and laughing
They crank the music loud
And prowl the streets for chicks.
Jocks decked out in colored letter jackets
Congregate like rat packs roving the streets
They hit the fast food joint
And gluttily wolf the food down.
Wasted strangers, three boys and three girls
Flee the streetlights for the countless dark lanes
Partaking in the shared lust
They overheat with joy.
Nobody notices the teenage child
Sitting alone in his teenage room
For the music is blasting
And the sobs are very soft.

I Stand Alone

I stand alone
Violently
Rebelliously
Longfully.
I stand alone
Brilliantly
Painfully
Angrily.
Here I am
Alone
A swimmer on the oceans of thought
A dreamer on sun soaked clouds
A prisoner of excruciating logic.
There you are
Together
Thwarted by mindless tradition
Blinded by primitive myth
Choked by inner shallowness.
Who says you are supreme rulers of right?
Who says you are crusaders against night?
Not I
For I stand
Where I damn well please.
Who says you are the singers of truth?
Who says conformity is good in youth?
Not I
For I stand alone.

'Tis better to stand alone
Than not to stand.

Too Late

She breathed.
She ate.
She coughed.
She cry.
She ran.
She laughed.
She loved.
She fly.
She slept.
She dreamt.
She sought.
She try.
She hurt.
She clutched.
She pulled.
She die.

Did she think the world would stop?
Did she think she'd become queen?
Did she believe she'd wake tomorrow?
Didn't she know it could not work?

A cry for help and then a shot
　　　Leaves the cry unheeded.
Attention dies in a few days.
　　　One must feel she is cheated.
Life goes on just as before
　　　Except a life is wasted.
All that's recorded in the book of life
　　　Is one more name deleted.

Did she understand?

Could she comprehend?

The meaning of the word

Final

Eccentricities

Splendid fits of sizzling madness
Burst over me like crashing tides
Spiraling me to unseen heights
Where poetry is the only expression.
Fleeting clouds strike my pen
Which strokes the paper in sloppy speed.
One thought immortal, one moment untouched
One notion forever engraved in time.

The Sky is Gray This Morning

The sky is gray this morning
A peaceful, uniform gray that fills all cracks
and crevices.
As I walk, a gentle breeze blows back my hair
And a bird's quiet song floats in the air.
6:30 says the clock-tower.
The coolness of the air I breathe into my lungs
Inspiring
Refreshing.
The buildings, usually threatening, seem to slumber
at this hour
Dozing on their gray pillow
At peace, at last.

The poets are out a-wandering
Enjoying a peaceful high.
Sometimes, I'll meet up with one.
Solitary and wispy, she'll float by.

My mind thinks nothing.
It has no thoughts to think
Except of how pleasant this is.
It has no challenges to meet.
It has no arguments to rebuff.
My mind is gray this morning.

I Strip in the Arena

I strip in the arena.
As my garments fall to the floor
Some will jeer and some will cheer
Some will laugh and some will freeze
Some will turn away.

Turn the spotlight on me.
See every part I have exposed.
I am naked, beautifully naked
And I breathe free and easy.

Should I see another stripping
Should I see another naked
I will jump and shout with glee
For he or she's like me.

We'll both run to the other
And throw our arms around each other
And feel the other's flesh against our own
And know that we are free.

Either the world will be converted
Or we'll be arrested by the cops.

The Lines All Rhymed

The lines all rhymed so good tonight.
The rhythm fell like rain.
My words expressed without a fight
My sorrow and my pain.
The inky tear has now been dropped.
I've spoken with my friend.
I feel as if the pain has stopped
And all is clear again.

For Patti

In the morning
A simple breath is taken
A breath of purity as the sun rises aloft
A breath of goodness for the kind earth's running waters
A breath of joy in the tingling scent of pines
And a breath of love . . .
love . . .
Love for nature's splendid trees
Love for its cool refreshing breezes
Love for its soft and simple flowers
And love for you my dear
As natural as the rivers.

In the morning
As the dew sprinkles the ground
I'll breathe the dawn's awakening chill
And think of you and I.
(In my arms, I'll hold you close
With my lips, I'll kiss your cheeks
With my fingers, I'll touch your hair
If only in my mind.)
I love the birds' melodic singing
I love the scent of a rain-drenched forest
I love the flight of a windblown leaf
And I love the girl who touched me:
More beautiful than the stars that shine
More precious than the dew that falls
More peaceful than the dove that flies
More natural than the sun

This is the girl who my heart flutters at the tender thought of
This is the girl that trembles my hands
This is the girl I weep for
(So very far away)

In the morning
A simple breath is taken
A breath of hope and joy and laughter
A breath of love and nerves and tears
A breath of simple fascination and slight anxiety
(What is this beauty I've encountered, this feeling, this
inspiration?
What is this I experience?
My God, is it . . . ?)

In the morning
A simple breath is taken.
All is peaceful
And all is good.

2

(Look! I think the sun is rising!)
Piercing the haunted trees
So glorious, so thrilling
Comes the new day's first golden rays
To dry the nighttime's tears.
(Celebrate! A new day has begun!
May this day be a joyous and beautiful one for all!)

For Patti II

In the misty morning,
Images, apparitions, fantasies play before my eyes.
At noon, I will see clearly
The apparitions having faded
The fantasies having fled.

Somewhere in the early morning breeze, I feel an
inspiration.
The dew of love is spread upon the grass.
I feel its tingling moistness.
The sun (ever elusive time) steeps its way above
the east.
It will rise further, further yet.
What will it show to me?

At noon,
The haunted trees will be free of their cover
The butterflies free of the cold.
A million different birds will be singing a million
different songs
A million songs for lover's ears
A million enchanting songs.
Will one be sung for us?

In the misty morning, while these thoughts I contemplate
The sun rises a little bit further
The mist recedes a bit.

For Patti III

Patti
soft, gentle, loving, touching
poetic fantasy
to feel her hand upon my face
to feel her cheek upon my lips
to feel her lips upon my own
ecstasy.
Oh Patti, please
Just one kiss and a touch of nature's all embracing joy
Would make me fly.
Would make me fly.

For Patti IV

An early morning rain came
So gentle and soft.
It made me kind of sad (it washed away the mist).
But then I looked up at the beautiful dripping leaves
And I put my hand up to my eyes.
An early morning rain came.

For Patti V

Late in the day
as the sun fades away,
the stars appear,
distant and pretty.

And at night, dreams, of course,
Dreams and dreams and dreams
     Beautiful dreams
     Enchanted dreams
But dreams nevertheless.
Oh Patti, if I could just share them with you
And let you feel the gentleness of my kiss
and the sensuousness of my caress
I know we could fly . . .

Oh Patti, I know our time will come
When we can run into each other's arms
And takes walks in peaceful duck pond parks
And kiss under the moon's pure white rays.
Oh Patti, someday, someday I know . . .

Until then, my dear, have the sweetest of dreams
May the sun's gentle rays light up all of your days . . .

And at night, when the stars are flickering above,
And you lay down that pretty head and shut those pretty eyes,
And your mind moves off to that distant beach
     I'll be running.
     I'll be running.

For Patti VI: As the Curtain Falls

There once was a girl, twenty, pretty, intelligent, deep
everything
She liked me, she got word to me, I was startled . . .
Alone again, I think.
Alone, alone, alone, always, always alone . . .

And I loved the girl who touched me:
More beautiful than the stars that shine
More precious than the dew that falls
More peaceful than the dove that flies
More natural than the sun . . .
(In my arms, I'll hold you close
With my lips, I'll kiss your cheeks
With my fingers, I'll touch your hair
If only in my mind) . . .
A breath of hope and joy and laughter
A breath of love and nerves and tears
A breath of simple fascination and slight anxiety . . .
to feel her hand upon my face
to feel her cheek upon my lips
to feel her lips upon my own
ecstasy . . .
(What is this beauty I've encountered, this feeling, this
inspiration?
What is this I experience?
My God, is it . . . ?)
Waiting for a letter from my loved one across the fields
These are the longest, loneliest hours of them all.
The mailbox is empty, day after day . . .
As long as you are there and I am here
Nothing can happen.
Absolutely nothing.

And I just kind of hang
See, I'm just kind of hanging here . . .
An early morning rain came
So gentle and soft
It made me kind of sad (it washed away the mist) . . .
If I could kiss you once, just once
I know I could communicate.
But, the distance prevents us
And someday, I know, you'll fade away . . .
I can't enjoy the scenery
I can't pursue a mockingbird
I can't launch forth a nighttime poem . . .
And, at night, dreams, of course
Dreams and dreams and dreams
      Beautiful dreams
      Enchanted dreams
But, dreams nevertheless . . .
'Cause I've never seen your eyes
I've never seen your mouth pronounce the words . . .
And I cried and cried and cried and cried . . .
No substance!
No truth! . . .
Tommy go insane lately . . .
See, I'm just kind of hanging here . . .
And the mailbox is empty day after day . . .
The tears roll down my cheeks because I feel afraid . . .
I cry and cry and cry . . .
Chaos, confusion, turn it away . . .

Why?

Tears . . .
Cheeks . . .
Hope . . .

Cry . . .

Why did I do that anyhow?

without her

the first move is
precarious, like a hummingbird
thrown from the nest who beats his first air stroke
and all of a sudden
is gone.

I Cry for Nations Caged in Red

I cry for nations caged in red
The eyes that cried; the hearts that bled
The grimy hand that grabs the ax
The back that lifts the grain filled sacks
The soldier straight who makes the round
The brain that quivers at a sound
The butcher sad who cuts the meat
The housewives bland who line the street
The stone officials in their roles
The labor campers' shoveled holes
The houses buried deep in snow
The fence that keeps the throng in tow
The voice that spatters out the views
The people watching daily news
The workers plodding, all but dead
I cry for nations caged in red.

My Dog

My dog only drank black water
ate what I discarded.
My dog always smiled when I patted him
ran when I whistled.
My dog, cheerful, playful, simple
was content fetching my slippers.

I couldn't believe when I found him out back
eating pieces of the sun.

The City of the Dome

In daytime
She's a respectable public servant.
The people she works for could never imagine
What she does at night.

The dusk falls
And she runs into the streets of the city of the dome.
Old newspapers blow through the streets, discarded
Today's news; We know; Who cares?

She dons her boots and make up
Waiting for the men
To come and tickle her panties with dollars
She'll do anything for them.

I've seen it so much.
I've seen the balding, three pieced businessmen
Wave their little wads and she goes jumping.
They'll take their fill of her
And leave her in the morning, chuckling.
She's happy; They're happy; the whole world's happy.

Right?

In daytime
She's a respectable public servant.
She decorates her office with stuffed animals
Donkeys; elephants; eagles
I run into her office, inquiring (fiery-eyed; on a crusade)
She looks over her horn-rimmed glasses
And hands me a newspaper.

The people she works for could never imagine
What she does at night.

One Morning in Weeks Hall

One morning, in fact it was
April 26, 1983 at 9:35 a.m. in 125 Weeks Hall
at University of Wisconsin Madison i sitting next to
some Geologist or soon to be geologist like he dreamed
of rocks his whole life said he wanted to be a
geologist since he was nine i couldn't relate but i
wished him well on the test ol' Professor Yawnlong
was handing back it was a biggie! and basically
it would determine if his grade point would be
high enough for him to get into geology school
so he could spend his time looking at rocks and
stuff and he handed him the test and he handed
me the test and Hey! An A! No sweat! and
i looked at him, his forehead was crinkled, his
hands were shaking, water seeped his eyes and
knapsacks zipped, books slammed and talk
and laughter cluttered the air in 125 Weeks Hall
at the University of Wisconsin Madison at 9:41 a.m. on
April 26, 1983.

party poems

i

laughter stretches from every direction
house is hot, beer slightly warm
squeezing and scrunching through bodies, i
want to get laid tonight.
through the smoke itching my eyes
forms move hesitant,
12:00 and screeching music
blasts through aching speakers
erratic spurts, electric jumps
bass pounding incessantly
ears cry in chaos
bodies cry in lust.

i, skillfully searching, spill, through the smoke
inattentively
brews of heavens past.
apology
brings me pair
of chestnut brown eyes
penis jump, saliva rivers flow
(inside)

smiling face, tiger tan
silently touching, hand in hand
dive and swerve, escape the throng
fever rising, heartbeat strong
up the stairs, to the right
now to the left, outta sight.

ii

moonlight
reflecting on her smile
on the eyes, delighted
on the breasts, pointed
on the giggles, naughty
on the . . .
she wants it.
brain   cluttered
fingers   twitching
mouth   embracing
hands   grabbing
i   shivering
sweating   licking
            oh!
        rushing on
        grabbing ass
        coming, coming
      oh!   oh!
      want   body
      mouth   dripping
      loins   bouncing
O!   cock   coming   O!
    coming coming coming

through the floor
              pulsating tune beat beats to the frenzied drone
tales of thousand lands
                              mingle
wasted folks wishing
                    searching, grabbing for
that dream.
                              oh!
and me!

iii

my body around her, wrapped, like a million dancing neurons
my lips spreading their kisses upon those titillating mounds of breast
i play tongue nipple.
i see her exercise dimmed eyes, looking a little weary
my penis relaxes in the heavenly aura, my head in flight.
now that i have flesh on my flesh, all my pillow morning dreams
are here
i have her ass in my hand if i want it
i have her tits in my mouth if i want them
i have a whole woman under my bones, like an amusement
park of erotica.
she grimaces and pushes me away
she wants to go out and drink.

iv

shots of vodka lined
clear   pure
i want them in my throat.
buzzes bash my head
i tell it to the guys.
dilating pupils
i feel
Proud.

V

like scott wicked telling jokes obscene wildly laughing
eyes blood like shooting flames fuck spit wench from lips
and wick (dan) agreeing with scott head floating half
thoughts in hysterical air eyes blood like flashing cop cars
and rick car keys like anguished delight looking for
granada red, eyes blood like grenada
and tom (i) yelling "DRINK" at top of my lungs
urinating strange lawns to sight old ladies gasping
eyes blood like meaty virgins
singing mike "wasted tonight why go out to a bar"
to folk german old song like raspy rhinoceros blood
eyes like sunsets
and chris head numbed from all the excitement eyes blood
like autumn leaves hair curled like roman poet looking for a
beer and semblance of the sane not finding

like six alcoholic balloons floating above the city
or six gritty street fighters looking for something to smack
knuckles we
launch through the city in grenada red praying for
wenches and blind bartenders who'd take anything as valid
and are off around the corners above the clouds like sand
nothing but laughter and alcohol and love
looking for sex in the streetlights of passion
looking for excitement from the flashing sirens
we are alive! like torrents of rain in the spring
or a bouncing barroom dance in the rush hour of summer
whistling car obscenities, paking tisses on the sidewalls
and drinking, drinking, drinking
like a siphon of love in our tummies.

vi

back at the party like noise and misery
and screaming and music and spinning spinning
everything fades

vii

parched throat
aching eyes.
vessels striking my skull
            beating to my heart
"4:00" cries the wall
ceilings throb
slimy sticky sweat
let me die!

and up i sit, trembling
desperate
beer soaked carpet gag
                my nostrils
stale smoke mouth
muscles, penis sore
buddies, dead, tortured
breathing on the carpet
haunted by
thirst.
sprinting for the door!
grabbing for the knob!
fumbling, turning, running
stomach explosion!
convulsion throat!
peanut butter corn soup
splashing on the grass

i breathing
falling to my knees
falling to the ground
face smeared with dew

viii

eyeball-tearing sun
head watermelon
the kindly blue gentleman
"What's your father's name, son?"

Sonya

Sonya likes rainy days,
When the grayness folds itself around you
Like a wet leaf
When the wind touches your spine
Icy fingers bracing you
When your liquid brain fills up with ice cubes
Drunken martini heaven
The wild goose flies with oblong neck
And rubbers slosh the streets.

A Shot of Vodka in the Morning

A shot of vodka in the morning
      Makes you grow hair on your arms.
A shot of vodka in the morning
      Stiffens your back, broadens your shoulders
      Develops protruding pectoral muscles.

      Makes you grow a low gravelly voice,
      "Ha! Look at my pectorals."

A shot is poured by the reporter
of the early morning news as you get out of bed.
On the way to work, billboards pour you a shot.
The boss gives you a shot upon showing up.

You and the associates trade shots at lunch.

All afternoon, three bright colors
Dance and flutter before your eyes.

On the ride home, you take a shot from the radio.
It is colorless and tasteless
      But it makes you feel . . .

You want to steal hamburger from the feeble old lady
coming out of the supermarket.
You want to rip the tubes out of the old carpenter's
nose sucking breath in the hospital.
You want to point a gun at the head of the unemployed
father to get his family to move out into the street.

At home, while you recline in your easy chair,
The President winks at you through the television.
"Come. Have a shot with the President."

Freudian Night: Leaving Footprints in Vilas Park at 1:00 in the Morning

On my left,
outside a fence,
a patch of young conifers stand,
erect.

On my right,
swings hang idle,
seesaws rest on the ground.

Before me,
a trail of sloppy mud
slices through
the spongy grass.

I slosh alongside the trail,
chilled, on wet feet.

The hairs of my hands prick up
at the touch
of the cold wind.

(Radio towers
blink
in the distance
on off on off on off.)

A young man,
leaning on the railing,
watches
the disturbed waters.

A brown feathered duck
wades slowly away
from its mate.

Progress

Sun eats moon
and day takes night
as people run
offices and smoke.
Smoke and offices
run people as
night takes day and
moon eats sun.

in the beginning

i

that morning,

katy and i
in a dew soaked field

kneeling on
the grass

bowing our heads
to the fertile ground

silent.

we kissed the sun god
with our minds

as that morning orb
rose over a hill

orange and fiery.

ii

everything was fresh.

the birds sang
and the leaves were wet.

misty seraphic clouds
were dancing
over the lake.

we walked down
to the beach

and sat
with our buttocks
in the sand

enjoying our nudity
and composing prayers
to the sun.

late that afternoon,

while the waves were gently
caressing the lake,

we laid down
in the summer sand,
tongue touching tongue . . .

i gently slid
into her womanflesh
and with that spurt -

          a million children spread over the earth
          to do honor to the sun.

iii

"prayer to the sun god"

honor to the sun
prayer to the sun
the sun
              that spreads its light
              over the bountiful earth

give prayer to the sun
give honor to the sun
give thanks to the sun
the sun
the sun

elegy written in a country churchyard: 1983

the air
is teeming
with insects:
beetles
mosquitoes
waves of gnats.
they bump their little
bodies against
my arms, my bare legs,
my ankles.

a farmer slowly
rolls his tractor
in the direction
of his farmhouse.

an automobile
in the distance
kicks up dust
from a gravel road.

now the glimmering landscape
fades
from my sight.
the church mournfully tolls
the knell
of a parting.
the world becomes nothing
but darkness
and me
(insects crawling
all over me).

(words from beneath the rugged elms,
in the shade of the yew tree)

why

       the cock's shrill clarion?

why?

       every morning i was aroused
       and wearily plodded into the fields
       to spread the dung, to thrash the hay,

       and now i want to know

       why?

The Idealist's Song:
Walking the Streets of Neenah, Wisconsin

the night's swift air

        fluttering the pages of kant, thoreau

through the wind chimes of my imagination

        inspires me to try asking

            seeking

to feel air while houses rest in slumber.

houses rest in slumber, their TVs droning to
empty rooms,
their garbage cans eating paper,
unaware of outdoor wind,
caged in jails of lumber, glass, metal.

        i breathe deeply

what is this touch of dream

        that wakens pores across my brow?

this night's cool breeze

        that stimulates my senses?

wild images: a tear, a kiss, a home.

to inspire people

        to come share my dream,

i cry freely

        and breathe the air.

Black Cross with Red Sky

As the sun explodes,
ferocious winds
illuminate the sky
with blisters.
You are the only one who notices.

> (distant mountain villages
> cast their faint blue light
> onto the sides of the darkened mountains
> in praise of the Deity.
> the pleasant green meadow
> settles for the night.
> even your spouse lies in the grass
> enjoying the quietness of the field
> feeling the moist dew.)

ONE BLACK CROSS
superimposed on red sky.

one heap of ground.

And you climbing

an ascending staircase of granite slabs.

Through the blackness of its eyes
a battered skull stares down at you,
the left side of its jaw
crumbling . . .

Reaganomics Soup

First, take one part affluence,
ten parts poverty and mix.
Gradually pour in tax cuts
until deficit appears.
Sprinkle lightly with nuclear waste,
Add a half a cup of acid rain,
and five lumps of fundamentalism.

If pink film begins to appear at the top,
pour in a bottle of FBI.

Now, boil over blue conservative rhetoric
until soup becomes thick with profits.
Peel one ripe grenada.
Slice it slowly into boiling stew.
Add a dash of anti-communism.

After cooling,
Disguise with food coloring:
red, white and blue.

Serve with sincere expression.

The Old Man Begins Writing Poetry

Having been knocked out
in the drunk of night,
he awakes to his face
in the mirror,
top button pressing
against his neck
like a fist.

The toilet bowl faithfully
swallows
the secret sickly remains.

At work, while trying to concentrate
on the tiny incessant numbers,
he has flashbacks of
his face in the water
being destroyed then covered
with slime.

That night,
with his lower right eyelid
twitching,
the old man, age 23,
begins writing poetry.

Flies

Flies,
rubbing their paws
of the sticky sweet soda,
like so many stockbrokers
shuffling papers,
plan how to touch Tom next.

Itching and squirming,
Tom blocks out the sun
with his hand.
Flies explode
like popcorn or laughter
off of the orgasm-like
stain.

Tom slaps the table,
whispers an epithet
rubs the soda off
on his other palm.
Then, one cocky bugger
dares to rest:
The guts explode,
the germs go flying

and a dark cloud
blocks out the sun . . .

in the mountains of north carolina

breeze
tooth
awake
soft musty smell
rain on deck
fog
old shirt

deer head
mirror
red bushy hair
moustache on fat face
old overalls
bare feet

worn mat
damp deck
mountainside dawn

dripping flowers
scent of pines
soft, constant trickling
of tiny waterfall
bare feet
grass and mud
stretch

quiet melodies
from treetops
faint jagged rock
above high road
long winding trail

upwards
broken windshield glass
on bottom of hill
old truck

breathe

moist hair
cold feet
wet shirt
shiver

worn mat
wipe feet
soft rain
tapping
curl
beneath the blankets

snooze

nirvana

To Scott Van Zeeland, my nephew

Because Mom had left you
with the strange uncle with the
big nose,
you cried.

I held you close
and sang "Rock-a-bye" to you
in a low, relaxed voice
to let you know
I was all right.

Your blue eyes
stared at me.

Your right hand grabbed my ear
while your left hand explored my nose.

I smiled
and kissed your bulging cheeks
until you finally trusted me.

I can't describe the powerful feeling
except to say
I would have fought Wisconsin's icestorms
to protect you from the cold.

You sensed that.

When you fell asleep
on my shoulder,
I could feel you breathing.
It amazed me.

One moment, your whole body twitched
and I wondered what was going on

inside that beautiful small head.

When you heard the voice
of your Mom,
your head quickly turned
and your feet stamped on my thighs.

I delivered you safely
into her arms.

Single at 24

The sunset stings
this Saturday
and I become sick
with dreams.

The drapes close
and my body curls,
like an ant
on the verge of death.

Gentle absent fingers
caress me

and reactions race
up and down my skin

until suddenly,

kisses and tears
break out of me,
and I submit

to the emptiness.

Morning on a Tributary Which Flows Into the Eno

The hair-like front legs,
sticking out 45 degrees
on both sides of the head,
punch the water
as the water insect
scoot scoot scoots
upstream.
A widening circle
expands behind
with each punch.
The reflections of existence -
blue sky, green pines, purple
buds - are interrupted
by the energy
of the wavelets.

~

I wade
into a watery dream
of existence.
My body scoots among
the minute specks
of gray matter
which float on the surface.
I encounter a giant leaf:
yellow
with green splotches.
I scramble onto it,
splash over it,
then twirl and swirl
in the green trees and blue sky.

~

A yellow monarch
bounces over my head
and flutters insanely
in front of me
before crazily progressing
north.

~

My feet
are comforted
by the algaeic scum
which grows
underwater
on the rock
upon which I sit.
An oak leaf,
the color of dark blood,
rests next to the rock.
Strings of algae
clinging to sticks
swim in the underwater
current,
like creatures
from bad dreams.

~

A passing dragon fly doesn't know
there is no dry beach ahead,
only another river.
One transparent wing
feebly swings
in panic
above the water.
The other moistens
on the surface.

~

A fish leaps into the air,
splashing.

~

The water insect rests.
He floats slowly downstream.
The antenna protrude
into the sky,
feeling the air.
The water massages
his front feet, hind legs
and yellow underbelly.
As I shift my feet,
the insect punches upstream,
body and hind legs
gliding behind.

prayer to the moon

the drunken country boy
smiles to himself
as he wanders through the forest
then down the road.
the moon's gentle light
cleanses the ground,
relaxing him.
the damp smell of the air
lifts him higher than
the residual alcohol dream.
he thinks of revolutionizing
his life
to throw the people out entirely
and love the earth.
occasionally, a squirrel
darts loudly from its path
and he feels the leaves
like one would touch a lover.

a hawk's caw-caws fade into a nearby
field.
distant tree silhouettes
are braced yet sway with
the wind.
the forest, dark and alive,
stretches up on both sides of
the boy.
in ancient times, ghosts would fly
through the air.

in the slightly drunk yet happy
state of the boy

the earth has blended into a dream
quiet yet restless
from cicadas to scampering squirrels
to a distant hawk,
a scene of the most radical and
liberating movie,
or better yet ecstasy,
heaven on earth,
living it,
loving it,
laying down
in a grassy, breeze blown field
and hugging it
with his whole body.

something mystical
in a higher plane
ecstatical,
thoughts on women and philosophy
and astronomy and alcohol as a
beautiful drug.
his leg muscles feel full of energy
as he walks.
he swings his arms
into the air.

we are free.
we are alive.
we can reach heaven
without dying
without believing in god
or buddha or mohammed.
we are free to float in the
secret heavens

around us
never again
to feel alone.
the earth loves us
the moon loves us
the sun loves us
we don't need each other
if we love
all of the rest
of life,
breathing, growing
towards the moon,
towards the sky,
towards heaven.

The earth is unending
on all four sides
massive
compared to the boy.

"Just Friends" Having Sex

"You have a beautiful body"
I tell her
as my hands affectionately massage
the mounds and curves of her chest.

"You are a beautiful person"
would have irritated her, like my kisses,
or when I convey too much
affection in a hug.

She laughs as she plays with my erection
and excitedly feels my thighs.
Then, she grabs some exotic oil
and squirts it on my chest.

I lay back in her bed,
nude and physically free,
my gagged and bound emotions
struggling.

Escape Into the Snow

Snow darkness woods Wisconsin
White covers everything.
It is so exciting here.
The dark thoughts of an oppressive office
are revolutionized by
a pure white insistent dream.
Although it's cold, I walk outside
bundled up and happy.

~

A revolution is something silent
that takes place in the mind.
It comes from saying "no"
again and again and again.
It comes from insisting
on loving yourself first
and not being afraid
to play.

~

The rabbits run from me
and nervously chew their food.
Who is this clumsy bipedian?
they wonder.
They frantically collect things
reproduce and run in packs.
I relax, breathe the air
and feel inspired.

~

And so, I am a failure and I love it.
I'll never have to worry about nicks
in my yacht.
Give me the sky, the moon and the night.
I am a beautiful person
and I will not be punished.

Sunset Over the Gravestones

Bruno, Babbitt, Kinsella
The day is passing orange.
1902—1915; 1908—1982
The clouds pass in front
of the sun,
one breathtaking moment,
which is gone.

~

Bankers
storekeepers
barbers
mothers
lie here
teeth and bones.

It is a finish as brutal
as if they had been slaughtered in a day.

~

The years are so tiny
on the gravestones
in comparison
with the massiveness
of this day.

~

Darkness overtakes the sky
and the day leaves
like a temporary dream state.
For me, a sunrise
will follow this sunset.
Live. Be free. Be happy.

502